The Kids Are Gone, Lord, But I'm Still Here

The Kids Are Gone, Lord, But I'm Still Here

Prayers for Mothers

Betty Westrom Skold

AUGSBURG Publishing House • Minneapolis

THE KIDS ARE GONE, LORD,
BUT I'M STILL HERE

Library of Congress Catalog Card No. 80-67801

International Standard Book No. 0-8066-1863-9

Photos: Paul Schrock, 14, 48, 78; Strix Pix, 22, 34, 68, 90; Camerique, 58; Jean-Claude Lejeune, 84.

MANUFACTURED IN THE UNITED STATES OF AMERICA

This book is for Carol, Billy, Jeff, and Tom
in gratitude for the legacy of lively memories
they've left behind

Contents

Preface

Brother Lawrence cultivated a good habit that he called
"the practice of the presence of God." He knew an available
God with whom he could share everyday problems, the God
of his tears and his laughter, a friend who was at his elbow
in the monastery kitchen as surely as he was present in
the chapel.

This book is written mostly for women whose children
are grown. The prayer conversations in it are addressed to a
friendly, weekday God in the certainty that he is willing
to have dealings with a motley collection of pilgrims, even
pilgrims like me. I believe God is close to the gentle soul
who is serenely ready for each of life's stages, but he also
holds in his love the one who must be carried kicking
and screaming into each new stage.

The practice of God's presence can be a tricky business
when a lively family is still thrashing around in the nest—
those years when a daily quiet time is just an impossible
dream. But when the crowd thins out, when the kids leave
home in pursuit of their assorted destinies, when the nest is
empty, then the practice of God's presence can take on
new vigor.

In childhood I think I half-feared the idea of God's
omnipresence. It meant, somehow, that he was always around

to check up on me. But now that same fact brings enormous comfort and strength—not only can I join in the great majestic prayers of public worship, but I can also spill out to him in private my thoughts and my laughter.

As you read these prayer conversations you may well ask, "Which way is it with her: Is she reveling in her empty nest, or is she hating it? Is she content with growing older, or is she the eternal schoolgirl, longing for another shot at adolescence? Is she hurting at the departure of her grown children, or is she glad to be out from under?"

To every side of every question, I would have to answer, "Yes! Yes! Yes!"

Just as the teenager stands with one foot in childhood and the other in maturity, so do I. I suspect we all do, or I shouldn't dare to confide in you. I have reached my 50s, but inside I am still 35 . . . I am still 27 . . . I am 18 . . . I am 10. I dare to believe that in back of almost every formidable churchwoman is a girl who once cried herself to sleep because she wasn't chosen cheerleader.

In no sense is this a "how to" book. Indeed, in spots it is more of a "how not to" book. When I make mistakes, I make some beauties. This book is about me, because a writer writes about what she or he knows best. It is about feelings and about God.

The details of my adventures of the spirit are probably not like yours at all, but I share them because, in the day-to-day happenings that are uniquely mine, I brush up against some universal experiences, experiences we all have in common. I have tried to make these experiences so real that you'll catch yourself filling in the names of your own children and your own friends.

You're right. I am inconsistent. I love my empty nest and I hate it. I am proud of my children and I tremble for them.

There are days of tears and days of laughter, and for every mood I know a God who listens. I hope you know him too.

Some thank-you's are in order: first to my husband, Bill, for his unfailing support and encouragement, and then to five women who love books and love life and who were good enough friends to be honest in their counsel. They are Lillian Larson, Louise Swanson, Carol Uecker, Angie Sorenson, and Lorraine Kent.

The Kids Are Gone, Lord, But I'm Still Here

The kids are gone, Lord,
but I'm still here.
Help me to remember that.

Every time I hug them good-bye,
remind me
that I count.

The mother in me
may be unemployed,
but I as a person
am still on the job.

At first I couldn't handle it.
I kept wishing it all back,
sentimental about even the dull,
backbreaking stuff.

"How long has it been?" I'd think.
"How long since I faced a Boy Scout duffle bag
stuffed with blackened sweat socks
and mildewed underwear?
How long since I've risen at dawn
to sub on the paper route?
How long since I've had to add a leaf
to the table?
How long since I've had to double a recipe?"

After all those years of more—more—more,
suddenly it was less—less—less.
Always cutting back,
every day a problem in subtraction.

Do you want the truth, God?
I hated it.

But you made me look around, Lord.
You showed me a whole world
hollering for help.

All around me
new ways to keep busy,
new people to love.

You showed me new reasons
to double the recipe.

Thank you for neighbor kids
who ring my back doorbell
and accept my licorice.

Thank you for brown-eyed Roberto
from Argentina,
who lived in our recreation room for awhile
and sang Spanish in the shower
and showed me how to bake empanadas.

Thank you for Adam and Emmy
and other small people
in the nursery at church
who call us Grandma and Grandpa
and ask for help with puzzles
and carry their blankets to our rocking chair
for comfort.

Thank you for friends at the nursing home

who show up for my Monday reading
with their walkers
and their wheelchairs
and their wisdom.

The kids are gone, Lord,
but I'm still here—
still busy,
still happy,
still doubling the recipe.

It was always easy
to blame the boys, Lord—
for the mud on the hall carpet,
the spatters on the mirror,
the light left on
all night in the basement.

Would they ever learn
not to leave the ice-cream carton
out on the counter?

"I'll have to remember
to tell them," I'd say.

It's humbling
to have them gone, Lord.

The house still gets messy,
and that baffles me.
I can't pin the blame on anybody;
I'm fresh out of scapegoats.

There's no comfortable explanation
for those toast crumbs
in the silverware drawer.

*I Blamed
the Boys*

It's Not My Assignment

Keep reminding me, Lord,
I'm not on
the selection committee.
It's not up to me to choose
the people my kids should marry.

Oh, I've had my ideas.
I really did like his looks,
and they say she comes
from a good family.
But let's face it, Lord,
I haven't been asked.
It's not my assignment.

I can be on the welcoming committee
when they stop by the house.
I can be on the kitchen committee,
in charge of popping corn
or heating pizza.
They'll even allow me on the cleanup committee,
stacking records
or picking up coke glasses,
but I'm not on the selection committee.

I can't play matchmaker, Lord,
but for the prayer committee
I don't need to be appointed.
This is just between you and me.
Would you stand by
and guide them in their choices?
Please, guard their happiness.
Bless their plans.

Everybody's going back to work, Lord,
and I'm running out of excuses.

Reentry

I've rearranged the furniture
as many ways as it will go.
My recipes are overflowing
four boxes.

The garbage collector
and the man who reads the meter
can do their work without my help.

I may be smart enough for the world out there, Lord,
but I'm not sure I'm brave enough.

It's the reentry that scares me.
I'm in a state just short of panic,
like my third try at the driver's test.
Reentry will take
more than a new hairdo.

There I'll be,
fidgeting in some anteroom,
surrounded by children in high-heeled shoes.

I'll be intimidated
by their new diplomas,
their air of confidence.

I'm not sure I can handle
the application blanks, God.

Name and address of last employer—
(Is he still alive?).

Last salary earned—
(They'll laugh).

Credentials—
(Sandbox supervisor?
Baker of pies?
Burper of Tupperware?
Room mother?).

Shove me out there, Lord.
Toughen my skin.
Make me brave enough for reentry.

I've Always Liked Gray Hair

I've always liked gray hair, Lord.
In theory, I still do.

There's a softness to the gray.
With a good cut,
it can look fashionable.
Gray hair can suggest
wisdom, dignity, serenity.

In theory
I still like gray hair, God,
but I haven't quite adjusted
to the strands of it
in my own brush.

Somehow I want to tell people, Lord.
I want to explain to each new person
how once it was dark and shining
and swung in a casual mass
across my shoulders.

That's vanity, isn't it, Lord?
Help me to deal with it.

Everybody gets lonely, God,
and today I'm feeling that way.

I'm Lonely

When Adam was lonely
in his paradise,
he turned to you
with his problem.
I'm turning to you too.

For Adam, Eve was the answer.
You created a new person.

But there are people
all around me—
good people.
It isn't a new person I need.
Or is it?

Create a new person, Lord—me.
And this time,
leave the self-pity out.

Show me a new battle plan
for each day's loneliness.

What's today's answer, Lord?
Do I work it off?

Do I find a matching loneliness
down the street
and put on my coffeepot?

Do I use my solitude

for reading
or thinking
or praying?

When I have only myself
for company, God,
help me to be good company.
Make me a new person.

Empty Nest, Indeed!

Empty nest, indeed!
Oh, the kids have left home
(well—almost),
but there's one thing
nobody told us—
that kids leave home
years earlier
than their belongings do.

I hadn't planned on
all those years
of skis leaning against the garage walls
or Navy pea coats in the closets
or that seabox in the well pit.

I have dusted around
leather-work tools
and half-empty paint tubes,
Boy Scout canteens
and college textbooks.

At first when they left
it was "See you later,"
casually, like Hansel and Gretel
scattering bread crumbs.
They knew they'd be back
before birds could eat up the trail.

Now they are paying on mortgages
and planting shrubs
and refinishing woodwork,
and I am still custodian
of their childhood memorabilia.

I hang on to their leftovers
like the other half
of a redemption ticket.
I have muttered threats like,
"It's going out with the trash"
or "What's wrong with
their own storage space?"

But always I have postponed the ultimatum.
I am no more eager than they are
to make it final.

I guess I should thank you
for the clutter, Lord.
I should be grateful
for every tangible link
that reminds me
they'll always be coming back.

They Cross Over

They've grown tall.
They move away from me,
and I am Moses,
standing on Mount Nebo,
watching them cross over.

They have been stubborn,
sometimes angry,
rebellious.

They have tested me
in this exodus from childhood.
We have tested each other.

We have been hungry.
We have struggled together,
shared miracles,
and then dug in
for the next testing.

Now I stand on Nebo.
They stride into a promised land
where I am not allowed
to follow.

I stand on this high place
and taste proud tears.
I cannot follow,
but look at them—they've made it!
Praise God,
they've made it!

Am I a Little Late?

God of my strength,
is it a little late
to ask for courage?

You remember me,
the shivery little kid,
the fraidy-cat who backed away
from tree climbing, deep water,
and unfamiliar dogs.

I grew up, a taller coward,
pushing myself to face the city,
to hunt a job,
to tackle new responsibility.

Sometimes I still get scared, God—
afraid of being a has-been,
afraid of my shrinking importance.

I'm fearful sometimes
that my body will give out.

I'm afraid of coping
and fading
and dying.

I'm still looking for courage, Lord.
Am I a little late?

We talk sometimes
about the legacy
we'd like to leave
for our children
when we're gone.

*Legacies Go
Both Ways*

We have some family treasures—
the antique clock,
the glassware,
Grandma Fossum's chair.

The will makes
businesslike arrangements.
It's all signed and sealed
and notarized.

We'd like to think
we'll leave them
with some intangibles too—
some useful knowledge,
some strong word
they can trace back to us.

We'd like to think
something of us is molded
into their character.

But they've been the first to leave,
and each day we discover
the legacy they've left behind—
some of the things they've bequeathed
to us.

I don't mean faces
in the family portrait,
or piles of worn-out tennis shoes,
or pot holders they wove
at day camp.

Each child in turn
left us with some wisdom,
some savvy we could use
in handling the others.

Each of them left a stock
of childhood stories
that we've laughed about
and treasured in the retelling.

We've discovered that legacies
go both ways, Lord.
Something of what they are
has been molded into our characters too.

I can't make up my mind, Lord.
I wanted to grow up.
I prayed for self-control,
but I forgot to "say when."
Now I'm asking you
to take some of it back.

Oh, I admit
the "good old days"
weren't all that good.
Young can hurt too.

To be honest,
I can do without acne
and dating worries.
I'm not sentimental about outdoor plumbing
or the Great Depression.

But sometimes
I'd like to bring back
that dumb kid who went around opening doors
and poking into adventures
and kicking off her shoes
to feel dew on the grass.

Sometimes I remember
when every day had bounce and bristle to it
and I cared passionately about issues.

Don't let me lose
my sensitive edge, Lord.
I don't want to be anesthetized.
I want to feel scared,

*I Can't
Make Up
My Mind*

to feel excited,
to explode in outrage.

I don't want all the nubby textures
sanded off.

Give me self-control, Lord,
but, please, don't overdo it.

Bells on His Shoes

How old was he
on that first camping trip?
Two, maybe?
He was little, anyway,
so little we tied bells
on his sneakers.

Bells would warn us
if he was wandering too far
from the friendly fire,
the cooking smells,
the shelter of the tent.

Bells would warn us
if he was near swift water
or some deep thicket
where clumsy bears sniff the berries.

Now he is grown.
Tall and sure,
careless of old dangers,
he has ripped the bells from his shoes
and walked boldly out
where there are no trail markers.
He is out there, somewhere,
and we can't even hear the bells.

But you love him, too, God,
and you don't need bells.
You are always within earshot.
We can't do it any more, God, so would you?
Would you pull him back
from the edge of danger?

At church I'm a kind of fixture, Lord,
a part of
the permanent installation,
like the pew racks
or the candelabra
or the stained glass.

I'm a Fixture

If a sign-up sheet
is passed around,
my name is on it.

If a meeting is called,
I have a tendency to show up.

Through the years I have taken my turn
as Bible study leader
and clean-up chairman.

At bazaar time they've learned
I can't do stitchery or macrame
or hand-thrown pottery,
but I can arrive a little late,
toting four loaves of Swedish rye,
big and irregular
and steaming with old-fashioned fragrance.

They're used to me around church, Lord,
but I don't cause much of a stir.

My life story seems colorless,
a record of unspectacular sinning
and gentle forgiveness
and a quiet resolve to mend my ways.

A part of me dreams
of being a swift-footed messenger,
surprising somebody (anybody)
with some prophetic lightning bolt.

Sometimes I almost envy the fire-breathing convert,
the found sheep,
the reformed harlot with a story to tell
of lostness and hunger
and joyous acceptance.

But remind me, Lord,
that I'm not the star attraction.
You are.

Remind me my life story
isn't the one that needs telling.
Yours is.

Make me content
that in this place I have touched life,
candle-quiet
and cornerstone sturdy,
and nourishing as the sacramental bread.

Make Me a Better Friend

I look them up
now and then, Lord—
my widow friends.
I enjoy their company.
They're strong, warm,
interesting people.

I look them up
when I'm hungry for girl talk.

I call them
when I have an extra concert ticket
or when Bill is gone for the weekend
and there's a weepy movie on
that he's refused to see.

I do think of them, Lord,
but always at my convenience.
Maybe I'm letting them down
when they need me.

I have not had to learn
the taste of real loneliness
and it's too easy
to forget theirs.

Do they ever get hungry for homemade stew
but just can't face the leftovers?

What about when their house
is unbearably quiet
and there's nothing worth watching on TV
and the phone hasn't rung for three days?

Maybe there's a sick grandchild
in a town far away
they feel troubled about,
but there's no one around to tell.

Forgive my thoughtlessness, Lord.
Help me to become
a better friend.

I wore my new outfit
to church today, Lord.
Is anybody noticing—
now,
when I stand up for the hymn?

Coming up the sidewalk
I saw myself in the glass door.
I do think it's my color.
The skirt is the new length,
and I love the textured fabric.

I guess I'm like Minnie Pearl
with price tags dangling from her hat.
It's a little obvious.
I've got something new!

But is it important, Lord?
What difference does it make?
Going in to church with something new
feels good,
but it doesn't change anything.

Remind me, Lord,
it's going out that counts.
Send me out with something new—
a new concern,
a new fire,
a new resolve
to work at my discipleship.

Let it make a difference, Lord.

I've Got Something New

Let every worship bring
a fresh beginning.

Help me to shout it,
"Hey, look, world,
I've been to church!
I've got something new!"

He's big enough to leave home, Lord.
Make me big enough to let him go.

*Litany for
the Last One*

Almost overnight,
when I wasn't looking,
his shoulders broadened,
his feet tried a bolder step.

He's big enough to leave home, Lord.
Make me big enough to let him go.

Out there he will learn
that gasoline is not free
and that socks do not wash themselves.

He's big enough to leave home, Lord.
Make me big enough to let him go.

Out there he will find that an alarm clock works
as well as my wake-up call
and that some wounds can't be healed
with a Band-Aid.

He's big enough to leave home, Lord.

But here I am,
stuck with all this leftover advice,
this know-how that didn't get used up.

Make me big enough to let him go.

Here I am,
like a former ruler

the morning after a coup d'etat,
out of power
and not quite able to handle it.

Make me big enough to let him go.

I admit it, Lord. I meddle.
I violate that delicate boundary
between perpetual caring
and perpetual care.

Make me big enough to let him go.

But tell me, Lord,
why does it have to end now,
just when we're getting to the good part?
Now, when he's learning to find the laundry chute
and remembers to say, "Thank you,"
why does the curtain have to come down?

Lord, make me big enough.
Make me big enough to let him go.

Teach me that apron strings
are not a substantial lifeline.
Remind me that ties of parenthood
are meant to be done with a slipknot.

He's big enough to leave home, Lord.
Make me big enough to let him go.

We used to have
gypsy notions, Lord,
crazy longings for countries
we'd only read about,
urges to take off
for faraway places
on a moment's notice.

But the kids and the budget
clipped our wings.
The best we could do
was to hook the camping trailer
to the back of the station wagon
and lumber 200 miles
up the highway.

"Someday," we used to say,
"Someday when he isn't president
of the Lab Association,
someday when the car is paid for
and we aren't expected
at a nephew's wedding,
someday . . . ."

Now the kids are no problem, Lord,
and we can afford
the price of a ticket.
"Someday" has arrived,
but we've become somewhat cautious gypsies.

Before we go,
we stop the mail

We're Cautious Gypsies

and the newspaper.
We ask a neighbor to water houseplants.

We notify the police
and leave one light on
to fool the burglars.

We've had the will revised.
We pack drip-dry clothing and airsick pills
and a mending kit.

Overcarefulness gets in the way
of the adventure.
We're somewhat cautious gypsies.

You've given us traveling orders too, Lord,
but again overcarefulness
threatens the adventure.

"Go ye therefore," you said.
"Take off, and make disciples.
Go to where the needs are."

That doesn't have to be far, does it, God—
where the needs are?
Maybe across town
or down the street
or into the next room.

But we're cautious messengers, God,
as though we need a professional guide
and a visa
and a guaranteed reservation.

Nudge us
one more time, Lord.
Help us keep our eye
on the adventure.
Tell us to go.

There were important people
at the luncheon, Lord,
women who get
their names in the papers
and serve
on boards of directors.

They smiled at me;
they shook my hand
and said flattering things.

It felt so good that I pretended to fit in.
I nibbled at my salad
and returned the smiles
and said flattering things right back.

It was like I was seven again,
on our old front porch,
playing "Big Lady."

There I was,
teetering in Mother's high heels,
a purse almost dragging on the ground,
a hat falling down over my eyes.

I guess I called my sister
by some grand name
like Mrs. Porterfield
or Claudia Ashley.

Only back then we both knew
it was just a game,
playing "Big Lady."

Playing
Big Lady

We both knew we'd get tired of being that nice,
and that soon we'd be back fighting
about whose turn it was
to wash the dishes.

You know me, Lord.
You see my little pretensions
and you love me anyway.

But why do I play "Big Lady"?
Who do I think I am?

Help me to grow up
before I grow old.

In the Holy Land
we see them, Lord—
at Jericho, in Jerusalem,
near the Dead Sea—
cities piled on each other
like layers in a cake.

We visit the digs.
The archeologist's shovel
gives back to us
the pool of Bethesda,
Joshua's Jericho—
each civilization hooked together
with the memories of the one before.

My life forms a layer too, Lord,
built on layers of other lives.
I stand on the memories
of generations
who are a part of what I am.

In order to discover who I am,
it is good to learn about
those other layers.
I dig with a careful shovel.

There will be others, Lord.
Other lives will be built on mine.
But remind me,
my layer has meaning.
My life will be sifted and examined.
Help me build it well.

*My Layer
Has Meaning*

A Good Kind of Pain

I've lived awhile, Lord,
and pain has been
a part of the package.

I've felt growing pains
and birth pains,
pains of disappointment,
illness,
separation.

I have known the pain
of sending a son to war.

Now I'm getting older, Lord.
This is no time to ask that pain should stop.
But could some of my pains be growing pains?

If I've got to hurt,
make it a hurt worth having.
Please, no pains of stiffness or inactivity.
Keep my spirits limber.
May I hurt from stretching too far,
from trying too hard.

I think I can still take growing pains, Lord.
Try me.

Lord, where did I first learn
the Mary-Martha game?
Was it at a Bible study?
At a church women's convention?

What speaker first led me
to that house in Bethany?
Who asked the question,
"Are you a Mary
or a Martha?"

Everybody was solemnly playing,
so I did too.
Smugly I asked,
"Which kind of saint am I?"

Am I Martha—
conscientious, potato-peeling,
laundry-folding Martha?

Or am I Mary—
calm, ethereal,
aglow with devotion?

Am I Martha-saintly,
or am I Mary-saintly?
Which role fits?

To be honest, Lord,
I had myself believing
I'd be good for either role.
I'd stumbled upon the perfect balance

*Mary
or Martha?
Which Am I?*

between the practical
and the spiritual.

I conveniently forgot all those days
when I don't fit either role,
when I'm no kind of saint at all.

There are days dedicated
only to shopping for trifles
or chattering on the phone
or gulping up soap operas.

I'm done with the Mary-Martha game, Lord.
I think I'm ready now
for another step
toward discipleship.

Teach me usefulness, Lord.
Teach me gratitude
and love
and everyday kindness.
Canonization can wait
for awhile.

Thank you, God,
for every joy
that childhood
gave to them,
but thank you, too,
for every tough time
that taught them to be strong.

*Thanks for the
Tough Times*

When I see that they are able
to argue and then love again,
I thank you for backyard shouting matches
that ended with a grin
and a fresh game of Annie-Annie Over.

When a business deal
doesn't work out for them,
I thank you for neighbors
who used to walk right by
their sidewalk Kool-Aid stand.

When they lovingly strap
orthopedic shoes in place
or push a wheelchair
around the zoo,
I thank you for the gentleness
learned from a broken-winged bird
in a cardboard box.

When I learn
that their baby took sick
and that plans had to be cancelled,
I thank you for all those times it rained
the day of the big picnic.

As they stand bravely beside a new grave,
I thank you that
a bouncy little chihuahua named Gypsy
was once softly laid to rest
in our flower bed.

And so, Lord, thank you,
thank you for those
strengthening streaks of sadness
in the bright fabric of their childhood.

I think I'm finally
getting the hang
of church work, Lord.
I'm putting up
a sign that reads:
Let's make it potluck.

I admit it.
I'm changing my style.
Once I did nothing
but one-woman shows.

Nobody else could run the kitchen
to suit me.

The church school project
would fall apart
if I didn't do the whole thing
single-handedly.

If committee work was to come out right,
it was up to me
to take care of it.

I'd still be operating that way
if I hadn't discovered
potluck dinner parties at home.

I had always played superhostess,
flying from oven to telephone
to refrigerator to vacuum cleaner.
I was always limp with exhaustion
when guests arrived.

*We're Going
Potluck*

Then I found it—
the beautiful freedom of potluck.

Suddenly it was nice to know
that somebody else
was dropping chunks of fruit
into half-thickened Jello.

Somebody else was frosting a cake
or assembling a casserole.

And me?
I was serenely vacuuming the welcome mat,
hanging up guest towels,
lighting the pillar candles.

You know, Lord,
church work is fun again
since I've learned to share it.

Everybody does a little,
nobody has to do too much.

I'm not handing in my resignation, God.
Don't think I'm trying
to get out of everything.

The work of the church will get done,
but from now on
we're making it potluck.

Remember that prayer
I used to pray—
the one where I asked
for five minutes of silence?
My prayer has been answered, Lord.
Tonight silence wraps the house
like cotton.

It's quiet, too quiet—
like a frowning librarian
or a sign in a hospital corridor,
the one that says: Shhhh!

Remember how I used to retreat
from the kids' arguments
and their rock music
by going out to weed flowers?
Tonight I'm tempted to turn on
the "Top 40" station
and invite the neighbor kids in to holler.

Tonight I'd like it
if a basketball would only thump
against that spot above the garage door.

Tonight I'd just as soon
have doors banging
and horns honking
and phones ringing.

Maybe it sounds ridiculous, Lord,
but for old times' sake,
send me five minutes of bedlam.

It's Quiet—
Too Quiet

They're on their way, Lord.
Freeway 94, Highway 7,
County Road 18.
All roads lead to Granny's.

There are gingersnaps
in my cookie can
and stubby crayons in the box.

Now it's time
to set things up high—
toothpaste and razor blades
and heirloom vases.

I'll put things out of reach.
It's easier than saying no.

But keep me within reach, Lord.
I'm unbreakable.
I don't belong up high.
Remind me to stoop down.

Make me available for touching
and hugging
and reading stories.

Slow down my clock, Lord.
I'll take time for their "help."
I'll tie big aprons
under their armpits.
I'll wash their hands
and stand them on a kitchen chair
and let them punch bread dough.

The Grandchildren
Are Coming

They're almost here, Lord.
Make me ready.

Only the Wish List Changes

The coveting hangs on, Lord.
Only the wish list changes.
At every age, there is envy;
at every age, the torment
of something out of reach.

I've grown out of
yesterday's longings, God.
I no longer covet
my neighbor's doll buggy,
my neighbor's prom dress,
or her cashmere sweaters.

I'm not bothered anymore
by my neighbor's designer wardrobe
or my neighbor's patio furniture.

Oh, I'm still coveting,
but I've got a new wish list.
The commandment needs revision.

Chisel these words on stone tablets, Lord:
Thou shalt not covet thy neighbor's suntan.
Thou shalt not covet thy neighbor's waistline.
Thou shalt not covet thy neighbor's
shining-eyed eagerness
for tomorrow.

Are You Expecting?

They didn't even know
I was watching, Lord,
but I was.

I saw the tall, red-haired girl
take a good look at
the one in the loose overblouse.
I saw the hesitation,
the half-smile,
then I heard the question,
"Marty, are you expecting?"
and the answer, "Does it show?"

You know, Lord,
I almost wanted to be in on
the hugging that followed.
Marty was me, 20 years ago,
and I could remember the feeling.
I could remember wanting to stop strangers
and tell them, "It kicked! My baby kicked!"

It's not just loving babies, Lord.
It's not that I'd care to go back
to Pablum and two o'clock feedings.
It's just that expecting makes a person feel alive.
There's a sense that tomorrow
offers unlimited possibilities,
that the future is brimming
with good surprises.

In some way
I'd like to keep right on expecting, Lord,
and I'd like it to show.

Once in awhile
the subject comes up,
"Isn't the house a little big now?
Maybe we should sell."

Postcards from the realtor
offer painless transition.
The man invites himself over
to put together
a free appraisal.

A moving company
peddles its usefulness.
It promises to wrap glassware
and box books
and tape the refrigerator shut.

Being uprooted might be a good idea
for a seedling
that sprouts overnight
and loosens at the first bite
of the hoe,
but it's not for me, Lord.

Like searching fingers
my roots have learned
to know this place,
twining around the rock of it,
digging deep,
pushing, clutching, hanging on.

It's home, Lord.
I've brushed three coats of paint

Maybe We
Should Sell

on those basement walls.
I know exactly where to look
for the pink nose of the rhubarb plant
poking out in the spring.

I've shopped for carpet
and chosen wallpaper
and scraped varnish from woodwork.

I know we can't keep it forever, Lord;
we can't pin our hopes
on a piece of real estate.
Gardening and lawn-mowing and home repairs
could lose their charm.

But while we're strong enough,
until something else looks interesting,
let us keep it, Lord.

It's home.

It's a good feeling,
being able to pay the bills,
but, Lord, I'm afraid
money is becoming
important to me.

I buy one thing to wear,
and suddenly two other things
don't match.

I'm entertained by a friend,
and then I wonder
if my house is good enough
to ask her back.

One trip is a great experience,
and secretly I begin
to think about a tour
of the world.

A smooth young man
with a conservative necktie
prescribes a tax shelter,
and it doesn't sound as devious
as it did last year.

Save me, Lord, from creeping greed.
Remind me of its ugliness.
Show me a better place
for storing up my treasures.

Money
Is Becoming
Important

Another meeting today, Lord,
another name tag.

Sometimes it's shaped like a dove,
sometimes like an autumn leaf
or an anchor,
but it's always there
so someone can know my name
for a moment
before moving on.

By the hundreds
we brush by each other,
drink coffee standing up,
exchange pleasantries,
then move on to another meeting,
another name tag.

You moved among the multitudes, Lord.
You managed to love them
and heal them.
You even miraculously
stretched one lunch
and invited them all to stay.

But wasn't it nice
to get away from all that?
Wasn't it good
to leave the crowds behind
and relax with a few friends,
just 12 friends
whose names came easily to mind?

*Another
Name Tag*

Thank you, Lord,
for my friends,
my close friends,
who don't need get-acquainted games.

Thank you for every friend
who uses my back door
and feels at home at my kitchen table.

Thank you for every person
who doesn't need to read
my name tag.

Pride—
I know it's on your
"seven most deadly" list, Lord.

I know that
out-and-out bragging
is forbidden.

But you were talking
about children—
and grandchildren?

If you were,
I'm in big trouble.

You've seen the grown children
in my wallet, Lord.
I am a little proud
when one makes the dean's list
or another lands a new job.

I always think
a few friends will want to know
about my son's thoughtful gesture
on Mother's Day.

It was your hand
that fashioned my grandchildren, Lord.
You gave them that mix
of beauty and wide-eyed wisdom,
so don't you agree
they have star quality?

*I'll Try
to Hold Back*

Look at Jenny's crayon sketch
of the farmhouse
on my refrigerator door.

And did you hear
what Paul told
his Sunday school teacher?

And have I mentioned
Kristen's gutsy cheerfulness
in the face of her disability?

I'm counting on you
to understand my feelings, God.
It was your voice, wasn't it,
that spoke from the cloud,
"This is my beloved Son."

Of course you had a lot
to be proud about.

Maybe the rest of us
should hold back a little.
I'll try, God.
I really will try.

I seem to be
bucking the trend, Lord,
but I just can't say,
"We're cutting back
on the Christmas card list."

The cards pile up
and spill over the sides
of the basket.

The logic is all with the list-slashers.
The 3¢ stamp has become the 5¢ stamp,
and the 6, and the 13,
and the 15.

But for a bright, perforated strip of stamps
I can call back to memory
all of those years.

Everyone I have ever liked
passes by in review
as I sit at the table,
addressing the cards.

In scribbled notes we tell
how we feel about Christmas
and how we feel about each other.

For the price of a stamp I can remember
the flavor of Edna's almond coffee cake
and her steamed cranberry pudding.

We seldom see him anymore,

*Cutting
the List*

but for the price of a stamp,
once a year we can remember
the gentle man
who taught our boys
to build a better campfire.

For the price of a stamp
I can recall to mind
the stillness in the college chapel,
the pig-tailed girl who strummed a ukulele
at Girl Scout camp,
the brown-bag lunches
in a supply room on the 12th floor
of a Chicago skyscraper.

With a Christmas card
we remind each other
that we are friends,
and that we are friends of the Christmas Child,
and that friendship is not easily
crossed off a list.

I Believe in the Communion of Saints

The service is over, Lord.
Again I have spoken the words,
once again I have
experienced the words,
"I believe
in the communion of saints."

I have exchanged smiles
in the narthex.
I have stopped to press the hand
of an old friend
back home from Arizona.

Bill's hand and mine
have held the same book.
We have sung together.
We have joined voices with John Wesley,
with Martin Luther,
with St. Bernard of Clairvaux.

Kneeling at the rail,
a thin wafer melting on my tongue,
again I have found
the communion of saints.
I have sensed a bond with those
who have died in your love—
my mother, my father,
my college friend, my grandson.

Praying the prayer of the church,
I have been linked with familiar names
on the hospital list,
the bereavement list.

Finally the benediction—
I have bowed and remembered
each of my children by name.
My thoughts have spanned the miles,
laying a hand on each head.
"The Lord bless them and keep them."

Thank you, Lord,
for this love,
for this linkage,
for this communion of saints.

When turkeys or chuck roasts
are on special,
we put some in the freezer
for when the kids come home.

Thank you, Lord, that this time
they all wanted
to touch home base
on the same weekend.

Billy and his family
got here first,
with carpenter tools in his pickup
in case he had time
for that door that needs fixing.

And then Carol's family—
the Volkswagen piled high
with security blankets and suitcases
and one springer spaniel.

And Tom was home between semesters—
sleeping off his finals,
phoning his high school friends,
borrowing the car for countless errands.

Jeff's family came Saturday night,
the grandchildren dragged out the old toys,
and we all played a crazy game
and drank coffee
and stayed up 'til midnight.

Thank you for a good Sunday, Lord,

*Home for the
Weekend*

for three generations of us
crowding the church pew.

Thank you that they like me well enough
to hang around the kitchen,
visiting,
sampling the dinner.

Thank you that they offer
to drop ice cubes in the glasses
and cut up carrot sticks
and grate cheese for the au gratins.

Thank you that my nerves
are reasonably sound
and that my arches
are quite strong.

And thank you, God,
for the tireless efficiency
of my electric dishwasher.

How I loved those parts
in my childhood books
where a frontier family
got ready for winter.

I felt safe with them
as they preserved crocks
of fruits and vegetables,
hung ham in the smokehouse,
buried potatoes in the root cellar.

I loved it, too,
when my mother
did her canning—
sweet and spicy smells
from steaming kettles,
tomatoes dunked in boiling water
until the skins slid off,
the taste of sticky foam
skimmed off the bubbling jelly.

"Putting up" fruits and vegetables
wasn't just survival insurance.
It was one way
of hanging on to summer
during the long months of winter.
A person could believe
in summer's reality
if you could look at bright fruits
and taste their sweetness.

Memory is like that too.
It is a way of "putting up"

*Hanging
On to Summer*

life's warmest experiences,
a way of saving happy times
so they can be enjoyed again.

Thank you, Lord,
that my shelves are stocked
with memories,
my survival insurance
against the cold.

I think I could use
an angel, Lord.
Not one to guard my sleep.
My sleep is in good shape.

I need an angel
like those in the Bible,
the ones who said,
"Get a move on."

To Peter in jail
the angel said, "Rise quickly!"
To Joseph in a dream,
"Go quickly!"
To Philip, "Arise and go."

A siren voice from somewhere else
coaxes me,
"Take it easy.
Prop up your feet.
Plop the recliner down.
Urgency is no big deal."

Send me an angel, God,
an angel who will hand me a parking ticket.

Send me an angel
who will shake me awake,
pull me to my feet,
and tell me, "Get going!"

I Need an Angel

I walked right by the closet
where I knew Jenny was hiding, God.

I knelt down
and peered under the bed.
I moved a chair
and looked behind it.

Then I said to myself
in a louder-than-usual voice,
"Where could she be?"

And Jenny crouched there,
believing I had not found
her hiding place.

For Paul I have been a puppy
and a dinosaur,
and for Kristen
I have played
doctor or teacher
or bus driver.

With the grandchildren,
I pretend to be somebody
that I'm not,
and it's harmless, Lord.

But when I pretend for adults,
I'm not so sure.

The doorbell rings,

*Find My
Hiding Place*

so I turn off the soap opera
and switch to the classics.

Or I nod my head
and smile in agreement at a party,
not wanting to admit
that I haven't heard what was said.

When guests are expected,
I hide the catsup bottle
and the dog's dish.

I catch myself
playing different roles, God.
With one group
I'd like to seem prim and virtuous.
For another I'd like to appear
worldly and sophisticated.

And soon
the person that I really am
becomes lost in the role playing.

Find my hiding place, God.
Tell me it's time
to stop pretending.

I've discovered something, Lord.
Teenagers don't have a corner
on peer group pressure.

At meetings I find myself
looking around nervously,
wondering,
"Is anybody else
wearing a pantsuit?"

And yesterday
I didn't quite dare
buy a sassy bumper sticker.
I could just feel my peer group
peering at me.

I thought that conformity
was kid stuff,
but look at me.
My peers have got me
eating my sandwich with a fork
and giving up on
the younger generation.

Give me gumption, God.
Help me to resist
this peer group pressure.

*My Peer Group
Pressure*

We're down to two now, Lord,
but two is not a bad number.

It's about time
for my engagement ring
to be remounted,
and our open stock china
is no longer available,
and bath towels
from the bridal shower
have become cleaning rags.

But the marriage itself
has endured.

Being six was interesting.
Those were stimulating years,
but there are good things
about being two, Lord.

We have more time now.
We have long talks by the fire,
and we go walking after supper,
and we don't have to worry about
behaving in front of the children.

It's not bad being two.
We enjoy cooking Sunday breakfasts.
I keep an eye on the bacon
while Bill cracks the eggs.

And when we play cribbage,

*Two Is Not a
Bad Number*

both of us taste victory
no matter who wins.

Two is not a bad number.
We've finally discovered
the butcher sells
other cuts besides hamburger.

Our life is like a jigsaw puzzle,
less bewildering now,
with fewer pieces left.
We begin to see the picture better.

The basic pattern is set,
and we've discovered it's a little late
for making each other over.

Thank you, Lord, for Bill,
who remembers anniversaries
and shops for valentines
and carries candy in his pockets
for the grandchildren.

Thank you for Bill,
who goes out in the snow melt
to poke radish seeds into soggy ground.

Thank you that when I yell too much
at a hockey game
or stumble on the liturgy
in church,
Bill doesn't pretend
I'm with somebody else.

We're down to two now, Lord,
but two is not a bad number.

My friend has died, Lord,
and neither my tears
nor my rage
can budge the heavy door
that has slammed shut
between us.

Mourning is necessary for me.
I grope for a way
to deal with my pain.

I turn to a commonplace pattern
I used to scorn,
and I discover wisdom in it.

I discover that it is important,
moving through a ritual of grief.

It becomes important
to stop at the mortuary,
to hug someone silently,
to sign the list,
to bake a pie for the family.

I go to church.
I bow my head
and remind myself that it's true.
God help me, it's true!
I fumble in my purse for a tissue.

I turn to your book, Lord,
to cleanse my sorrow
with the laments,

*My Friend
Has Died*

to brace my spirits
with the promises.

For her, you've promised joy,
and I do believe that.

For me, you've promised healing,
and that will come,
but not quite yet.

This life gone away,
this separated friend,
was something unique,
something irreplaceable.

For now there is no way
I can just get on with my life
without this ritual,
this ritual of grief.

Forth Like Arrows

Maybe the Persian poet
sent his children forth
like arrows, Lord,
but for a lot of us
it's been more like
tossing boomerangs.

Farewells have been temporary.
They keep coming back to us—
at least for awhile—
for an assortment of good reasons.

"I think I'll work for a semester"
or "Just while we're house-hunting"
or "My discharge papers are in order.
Can you meet me at the airport?"

For a lot of good reasons
they move back in for awhile
and sit at our table
and give us back our sense of family.

Thank you, God,
that they see this as a place
of love and shelter and welcome.

Thank you that in this house
they can still feel at home.

There is a myth that says
temptation is a problem
for the young.
I hoped that in middle age
I'd kind of grow out of it.

*An Equal
Opportunity
Business*

But I'm learning, Lord.
The devil runs
an equal opportunity business.
There's no age discrimination here.

Oh, the spectacular sins
have quieted down.
It isn't as tough
to resist their temptations
as it once was.

But I've found a whole new set
of temptations.
Now it's the ornery sins
that give me trouble—
sins like smugness
and hypocrisy
and judging.

The devil runs an equal opportunity business,
but you do too, God.

In my youth you saw me through temptation.
Please rescue me now,
one more time.

The class reunion was fun, Lord,
better than I expected it to be.

A Great Reunion

My prereunion diet didn't take,
and I fought off the temptation
to touch up my hair;
but it was good to find
that the others didn't look like
their yearbook pictures either.

The basketball captain was paunchy,
the cheerleaders had thickened at the waistline,
and the homecoming queen was graying
at the temples.

I had expected an evening of nostalgia, Lord,
remembering the alma mater with a lump in the throat,
sorting through scraps from a distant past,
but it wasn't quite like that.

Around the registration table,
in front of the washroom mirror,
we "girls" talked our heads off,
and the theme was "now."

Oh, children and grandchildren
in the wallets
got some attention,
but mostly we talked about
our own lives.

We've all survived

that jolting transition
from mother-in-chief to mother emeritus.

Nobody is just sitting around
feeling disposable.
We're all into new things.

Remember those little lists
under the yearbook portraits—
a set of accomplishments
to match each face?
(Band, 3 and 4; choir, 1, 2, 3;
yearbook editor, 4)?
It was good to learn
that every list has grown.
The resumes didn't freeze over
on graduation day.

And that commencement day speech,
"Get out there and lick the world"?
Well, that stuck, I guess.
Skills and judgment
learned in the mothering years
have become marketable items.

Miriam's back at teaching,
but now she comes closer to understanding
the child behind the desk.

From Girl Scout cookie chairman
to office manager
was an easy step
for Connie's organizational knack.

And Dorothy's boutique
had its roots in that needlework
she used to do at night
after the kids went to bed.

It was a great reunion, Lord.
We were all ready
to make reservations
for the next one.

We're ready to tear into
the opportunities
the coming years will bring.

I've got another 10 years
for lengthening the list
under my yearbook photo.
Stick with me, Lord.
I plan to keep moving.